vikings and their times

A BEEHIVE BOOK

This edition published in 1993 in association with
Simon & Schuster Young Books
Campus 400
Maylands Avenue
Hemel Hempstead
Herts HP2 7EZ

Editor: Penny Clarke

Printed & bound in Belgium by Proost International Book Production

ISBN 0 7500 8997 0

Photographs
Scandinavian Airlines: 10, 30 (B), 37
J. Allan Cash: 12, 46(T)
Photoresources: 16, 27, 46(B)
ATA: 26, 31
Norwegian Maritime Museum: 30(T)

National Museum of Antiquities, Scotland: 40
University Collection of National Antiquities, Oslo: 45
National Museum, Copenhagen: 50
Icelandic Photo Service: 54
Photo Ellebe: 55
Ashmolean Museum: 23

VIKINGS
AND THEIR TIMES

Michael Gibson

Beehive Books

Contents

The Vikings

The Viking Age lasted from AD 790 to 1100. At the beginning of this period, Scandinavia was divided into many small kingdoms. As the years went by, the states of Norway, Sweden and Denmark emerged. By the 840s, Vikings from Norway and Denmark were assembling large fleets and attacking many of the richest cities in Europe. These were ruthlessly plundered and then usually burnt to the ground.

At the same time, some Vikings, particularly Norwegians, were settling in the Scottish islands. From Norway, too, they made their way to Iceland, Greenland and finally America. This was a magnificent achievement for a people without compasses or charts (sea maps).

In the 860s, Swedish Vikings established themselves in Russia and began a flourishing trade with Arab and Byzantine merchants. Soon, Viking fleets were terrorizing the Black Sea and Caspian Sea as well as the Mediterranean and North Sea.

Although raiding continued, many Vikings settled in the British Isles, France, Iceland, Greenland and Russia. This book describes how the Vikings lived during the years of their greatness. The Vikings did not leave much visible evidence, but archaeologists regularly find objects which add to our knowledge. In addition, there are many superb Scandinavian poems and sagas.

The text and illustrations in this book are all based on these sources. Together, they give a picture of what it was like to be a Viking during the Viking Age. They also explain why the people who lived in the lands the Vikings raided were so frightened of the fierce warriors.

Terror from the sea

In 793 Viking raiders landed on the small island of Lindisfarne, off north-east England. They came without warning, attacking the monastery and stealing its treasures. They killed some of the monks and took others away to be slaves. Even worse, according to the Anglo-Saxon historian, Symeon of Durham, 'they trampled upon the holy places with their filthy feet and dug up the altars'. This raid was a warning of worse to come.

At the time of the Lindisfarne raid, much of Europe was ruled by Charlemagne, the powerful king of the Franks. As long as Charlemagne lived, the Vikings only dared make lightning attacks on his lands. When Charlemagne died in 814 his sons started quarrelling over his empire. They were so busy fighting each other that they could not defend themselves against the Viking attacks. The Vikings sailed up the great rivers of Europe, raiding and pillaging the peaceful countryside. These raids greatly increased the Vikings' power. For the next two hundred years they regularly raided and terrorized large areas of Europe.

▼ The Vikings pulled their longships up on to the beach then rushed to attack the monastery. The monks were caught by surprise for, as an Anglo-Saxon pointed out at the time: "It is some 350 years that we and our forefathers have lived in this lovely land and never before has such a terror appeared in Britain."

9

Homelands of the Vikings

The people we call the Vikings lived in Scandinavia, that is, present-day Norway, Sweden and Denmark. Although linked together in many ways, each country was independent of the others.

No-one is certain of the meaning of the word *Viking*. It may come from the Old Icelandic word *vik* which means *bay* or *creek*. A Viking was therefore someone who lurked with his ship in a bay. Some people think it comes from the Anglo-Saxon word *wic*, or camp, meaning that a Viking was an armed warrior.

However, the Scandinavians did not call themselves Vikings. This name was given to them by early writers. They probably called themselves after the area in which they lived.

▲ To seal a bargain, Vikings slapped hands. This still happens in France, Denmark and England.

◀ The long, narrow inlets along the coasts of Norway, Iceland and Greenland are called fiords. They are usually very deep but become shallower towards their mouths. They were probably formed by glaciers millions of years ago.

▶ Little land in Scandinavia is suitable for farming. Norway is very mountainous, Sweden is densely forested and Denmark has large areas of infertile heathland. Settlements were usually near the coast.

▲ One possible reason for the Vikings' expansion abroad was the shortage of good farm land at home.

▲ The skill the Vikings developed in building boats enabled them to make long sea voyages to distant lands.

Homelands of the Vikings

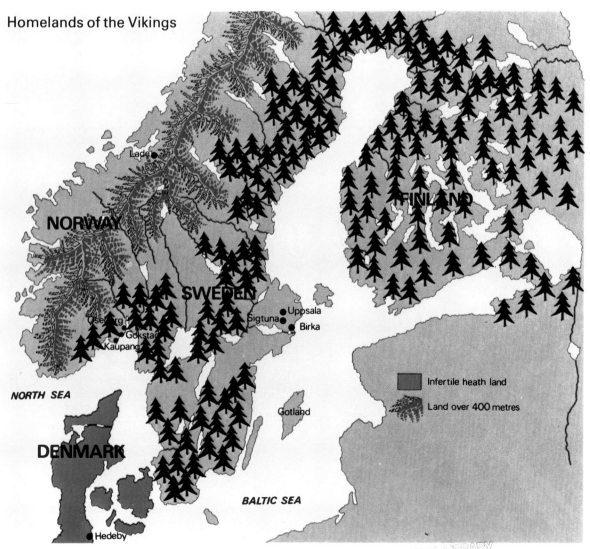

NORWAY

FINLAND

SWEDEN

Lade

Oseberg

Gokstad

Kaupang

Sigtuna

Uppsala

Birka

NORTH SEA

Gotland

Infertile heath land

Land over 400 metres

DENMARK

BALTIC SEA

Hedeby

The rules of society

Viking ranks

▲ Early in the Viking age, Scandinavia was divided up between many kings.

▲ Karls were rich freemen and farmers. They ranked midway between kings and jarls.

▲ Jarls were the most important group of people. They owned their own land.

▲ Thralls were slaves. Their owners had the power of life and death over them.

The family was the most important group within Viking society. People made decisions for the good of their family, not just for their own good. The Vikings were very proud people, so there were frequent quarrels between families. At the *thing*, or local assembly, a feud might be settled after both families had put forward their case. The *thing* decided who was to blame by listening to witnesses.

Sometimes people had to undergo an ordeal to prove they were telling the truth. Women might be asked to pick stones out of vats of boiling water. Their hands were bandaged for a time and then examined in public. If the wound was clean, they had been telling the truth. People who were found guilty were punished according to the law. Most criminals were fined or banished from the country.

▲ This is the site of the Icelandic Althing or National Assembly. It first met in 930 at the north end of Lake Olfusvatn. It was a combination of a law court and a parliament.

▲ If a man were killed, his family felt it was their duty to avenge his death. The feud might go on for many years.

▲ Sometimes quarrels were settled by duels. The duellists struck each other in turn until one gave in or was killed.

▲ Some feuds ended when the guilty party paid fines for the wrong done. The payment had to be made in public.

▲ Things *were assemblies of freemen where important matters were discussed. They were both law courts and local councils.*

Table of fines

All Viking goods were valued at a certain amount, like these dogs. Anyone caught stealing had to pay back the value of what had been stolen.

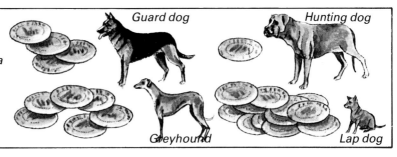

Guard dog

Hunting dog

Greyhound

Lap dog

Living on the farmstead

The long, cold winters and poor soil in Scandinavia meant that farming was very hard work. The Vikings' farms were usually small and the poor soil needed a great deal of care. The farmers grew barley and oats and, in some areas, rye. In summer they cut these crops with sickles and scythes. The ears of corn were separated from the stalks and stored until they were ground into flour. The farmers also grew peas and cabbages, and apple, hazel and walnut trees. The nuts and fruit were stored for use in the winter.

Cattle were as important as crops. In addition to meat, they gave milk which could be made into butter or cheese.

▼ The central point of this farmstead on a Norwegian fiord is the long house. The smaller houses are used as workshops or shelters for the animals. In summer the families tending the cattle in the mountains lived in rough stone or wood shelters.

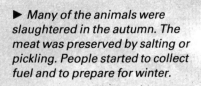

▲ When spring came the Vikings started to sow their crops. First they broke up the soil with hand ploughs or with ploughs drawn by oxen, then they sowed the seed by hand.

▶ Many of the animals were slaughtered in the autumn. The meat was preserved by salting or pickling. People started to collect fuel and to prepare for winter.

► In summer families drove their cattle up to the rich mountain pastures to graze. They made the milk into butter and cheese for the winter.

► In winter, the Vikings went hunting on their skis. Some, like this man, made tools and weapons out of wood and iron.

Store house

Long house

Byre

Forge

etable garden

Wood pile

Bath house

Home field

Homes of turf and timber

Most Vikings lived in rectangular houses with walls made of turves, upright timbers, wattle and daub or stone. The rafters of the roofs were covered with thatch, wooden shingles or turves.

In the early days these houses only had one room. The head of the family slept in a box bed, but everyone else slept on raised platforms running round the sides of the room. They cooked in a fire pit in the middle of the floor. The smoke from the fire escaped through a small hole in the roof. The walls were hung with weapons and sometimes with cloth hangings, showing the adventures of famous warriors. The floor was covered with reeds and herbs. There were no windows only some tiny slits in the walls.

The houses had little furniture. The head of the family had a special chair. Everyone else sat on simple benches or on the fur-covered platforms around the walls.

Later, the houses were divided into separate rooms. Although this made the houses more comfortable, they still remained dark, smelly and smoky.

Types of houses

▼ *The Vikings built many different kinds of houses. The design of the houses depended on the climate and the kinds of materials that were available. Where trees were plentiful, the houses were usually built of wood. The illustrations below show three types of Viking house.*

▲ *Curved-wall long houses were made of split tree trunks set in upright rows. The roof was supported by the walls and additional posts set at an angle to the wall.*

▲ *Stave houses had walls made of vertical staves or planks.*

▲ *Some houses had walls built of horizontal planks laid between vertical wooden posts.*

▲ *This turf-covered house in Iceland shows how many of the* Vikings' houses must have looked.*

16

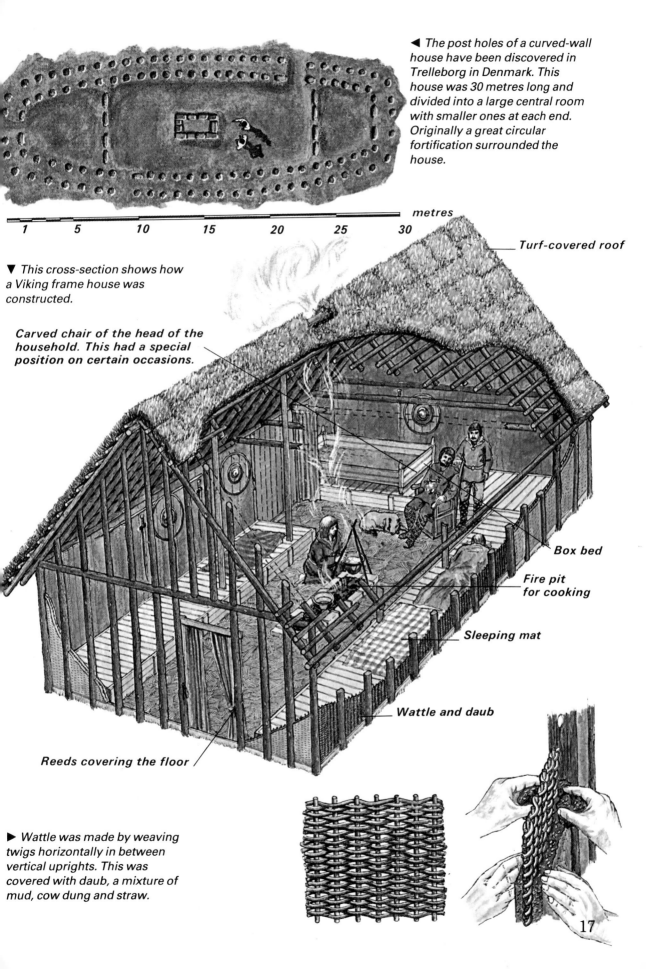

◄ The post holes of a curved-wall house have been discovered in Trelleborg in Denmark. This house was 30 metres long and divided into a large central room with smaller ones at each end. Originally a great circular fortification surrounded the house.

metres

1   5   10   15   20   25   30

▼ This cross-section shows how a Viking frame house was constructed.

Carved chair of the head of the household. This had a special position on certain occasions.

Turf-covered roof

Box bed

Fire pit for cooking

Sleeping mat

Wattle and daub

Reeds covering the floor

► Wattle was made by weaving twigs horizontally in between vertical uprights. This was covered with daub, a mixture of mud, cow dung and straw.

17

Family life

Viking families ate, slept, cooked and worked in the one room of their house. The two most important objects in the room were the fire pit for cooking and the loom for weaving. There were no cupboards. Belongings were either hung on the walls or stored in chests around the edge of the room.

Most of the cooking was done inside the house, though bread was sometimes baked in an oven outside. A typical meal consisted of thick slices of bread and butter, roast or boiled meat of wild boar, red deer, elk or even bear, with vegetables or fruit. They drank skim milk or buttermilk and whey, as well as beer and mead, a strong drink made from honey. The Vikings also used honey in their cooking, because it was their only form of sweetening.

After cooking, weaving was the most important activity. The women spun the wool and wove it into cloth. Then they made the cloth into clothes, wall hangings or cover-eings for the benches around the walls.

▶ The interior of a Viking home.

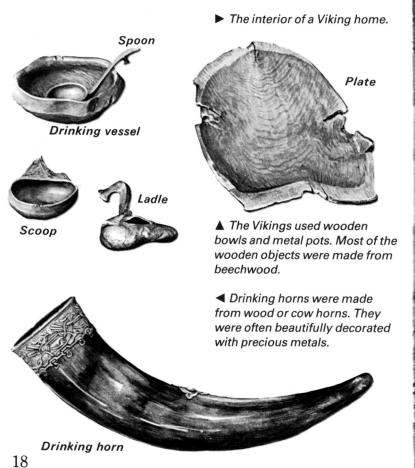

Spoon

Plate

Drinking vessel

Scoop

Ladle

▲ The Vikings used wooden bowls and metal pots. Most of the wooden objects were made from beechwood.

◀ Drinking horns were made from wood or cow horns. They were often beautifully decorated with precious metals.

Drinking horn

18

Clothes and jewellery

Before the Viking women made the cloth they had woven into clothes they dyed it. They used mineral or vegetable dyes of green, brown, red, yellow or blue.

The men wore long-sleeved jerkins or three-quarter length coats over woollen shirts and long cloth trousers. On their feet they wore leather boots or soft shoes with short socks. The women wore long woollen dresses and linen tunics down to their ankles. Their legs and feet were covered with thick woollen socks and soft leather shoes. Both men and women wore fur or woollen hats and cloaks when they went out in the winter. They fastened their cloaks with brooches at the shoulder. Children probably wore the same kind of clothes as their parents.

Gold and silver jewellery was popular. Archaeologists have found brooches, bracelets, necklaces, armbands and rings. Some of the jewellery was loot from raids on foreign churches and monasteries.

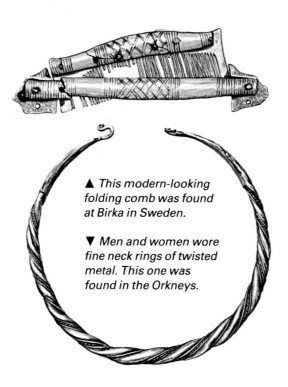

▲ This modern-looking folding comb was found at Birka in Sweden.

▼ Men and women wore fine neck rings of twisted metal. This one was found in the Orkneys.

▼ These people belong to a fairly rich family. Poor people wore similar clothes, but their jewellery and the embroidery on their tunics would have been simpler.

▲ This bronze brooch has been decorated with sheet silver. It was probably worn by a rich woman, between two oval brooches.

▲ This gold filigree brooch was found at Hornelund in Denmark. Women wore such brooches on each shoulder.

▲ This thistle brooch is a good example of Viking jewellery. It is made from silver and was found in Ireland.

21

Hedeby: the great market

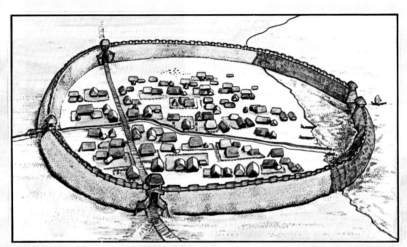

◄ Hedeby was surrounded by an earth wall. This was so high and thick that people had to walk through tunnels in it. There was also a strong sea wall made of wood. This protected the town from attack and provided shelter for ships.

Not every Viking lived in a tiny farmstead or village. Many lived in large towns like Kaupang in Norway, Birka in Sweden and Hedeby in Denmark. Hedeby was one of the most important towns in the Viking world. It was built on the Jutland peninsula facing the Baltic Sea.

The people of Hedeby were merchants and craftsmen. Some craftsmen made brooches, pendants and little figures, others were expert glassblowers, horn carvers and clothmakers. Viking merchants brought goods from Germany, France, Norway, England, Constantinople and Persia to trade at Hedeby. Arabs came from Spain and the Middle East to buy slaves because Hedeby was the centre of the slave trade. People from all over Scandinavia visited Hedeby to buy jewellery, fine cloth and other goods.

▼ Hedeby was built by the side of the Schlei Fiord. Excavations at the site give a good idea of what the town was like. There were at least two main streets paved with logs, with both large and small houses. Most of the houses had several storage huts or work places with their own well. These were all enclosed by a wooden fence.

25

The Viking craftsman

Not all Vikings were farmers or raiders, many were highly skilled craftsmen. Without the skills of the carpenters who made their boats and the smiths who made their weapons, the Vikings' raids would have been impossible.

Wood was one of the most popular materials in Scandinavia because it was readily available. Once the trees were felled, they were split into sections with wedges. The wood was then shaped with a tool called an adze. During the Viking age the Scandinavians produced magnificent wood carvings, both on their ships and on other objects.

To make a sword or an axe, the smith heated a bar of iron until it was white hot, hammered it and then plunged it into cold water to cool it quickly. He repeated this process until the weapon was hard. Fine weapons were highly prized and handed down from father to son.

▲ An axe decorated in the Mammen style of 960 to 1020.

▼ This carpenter's tool set was found in Sweden. The tools have changed so little that craftsmen today would find them easy to use.

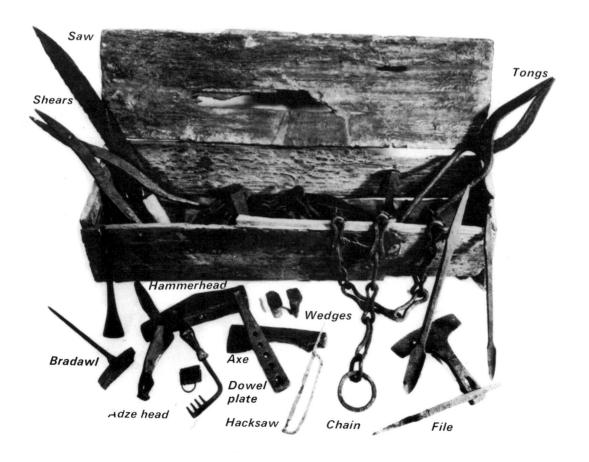

Saw

Shears

Tongs

Hammerhead

Wedges

Bradawl

Axe

Dowel plate

Adze head

Hacksaw

Chain

File

Decorating an axe

The Vikings often decorated their weapons with bronze, brass or silver. First the weapon was heated over a fire until it was black.

▲ The design was cut into the surface with a sharp instrument. Small pieces of silver, bronze or brass were rubbed into the hot grooves until they stuck.

▲ The weapon was put back into the fire, and polished with a long tool of smooth steel. This was repeated until the decoration shone.

▲ These scenes were carved in wood on the doorway of Hylestad church in Norway. They show Sigurd, a Viking hero, testing his sword on an anvil. The sword breaks and Regin, the smith, has to forge another blade. Sigurd uses the new sword to kill a dragon who was guarding some treasure.

Viking traders

Novgorod

Uppsala
Birka

Kaupang

Kie

Hedeby

Cracow

Prague

Mainz

Noirmoutier

▲ Rich Vikings drank out of
glasses like this one, brought
from Germany.

One of the most important routes developed by the
Swedish Vikings was southwards through Russia. Each
year the Vikings set out with ships laden with furs, wax,
honey and slaves. They sailed up the rivers of northern
Russia and carried their boats overland to the head of the
River Dnieper. They followed the river to the Black Sea
and sailed across to Constantinople, where they sold their
goods and bought wines and fabrics.

Other ships sailed down the River Volga to the Caspian
Sea. Here they met Arab merchants from Baghdad, who
sold them Persian glass, Chinese silks, Far Eastern spices
and silver.

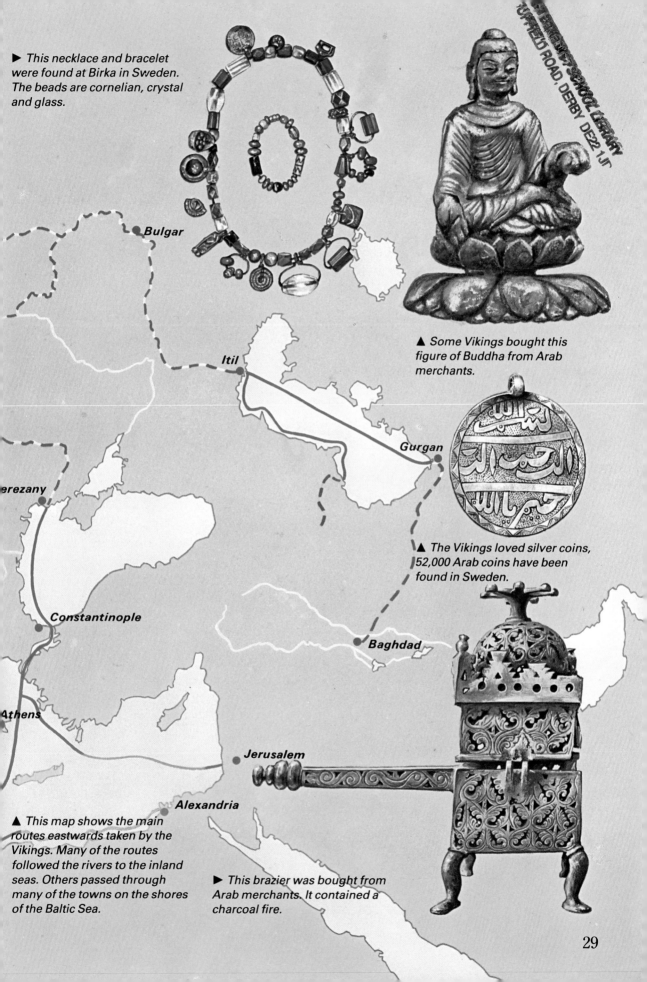

► This necklace and bracelet were found at Birka in Sweden. The beads are cornelian, crystal and glass.

Bulgar

Itil

Gurgan

erezany

Constantinople

Baghdad

Athens

Jerusalem

Alexandria

▲ Some Vikings bought this figure of Buddha from Arab merchants.

▲ The Vikings loved silver coins, 52,000 Arab coins have been found in Sweden.

▲ This map shows the main routes eastwards taken by the Vikings. Many of the routes followed the rivers to the inland seas. Others passed through many of the towns on the shores of the Baltic Sea.

► This brazier was bought from Arab merchants. It contained a charcoal fire.

29

'Steeds of the waves'

Viking ships were among the finest ever built. There were different types for different uses. One of the best known is the longship, a canoe-like warship. It was long and thin and sat low in the water. Its prow and stern were carved in the shape of savage animals which were covered in gold and silver, and flashed in the sun. When the ship entered port, its sides were lined with gaily coloured shields. These were removed when the ship put out to sea. The longship had one large square sail, which was usually striped blue, red or green. Each ship had a set of oars and was rowed in calm weather. The ship was steered with a large oar at the stern.

▲ This reconstruction of the Gokstad ship was sailed across the Atlantic in 1893. The Gokstad ship was found in a burial mound in 1880. It was not a specialized ship, and probably dates from the ninth century.

▶ The Gotland stone shows a Viking ship with a chequered sail. The Vikings were probably able to shorten or 'reef' the sail by pulling on the ropes hanging from the bottom of the sail.

◀ The Oseberg ship was reconstructed from excavated remains. The burial ship contained the bodies of two women and many of their possessions, including beds, blankets and chests.

How the longship was built

▼ *Viking ships were clinker-built. This made the hull flexible enough to 'give' against the force of the waves. These ships could sail in very stormy seas.*

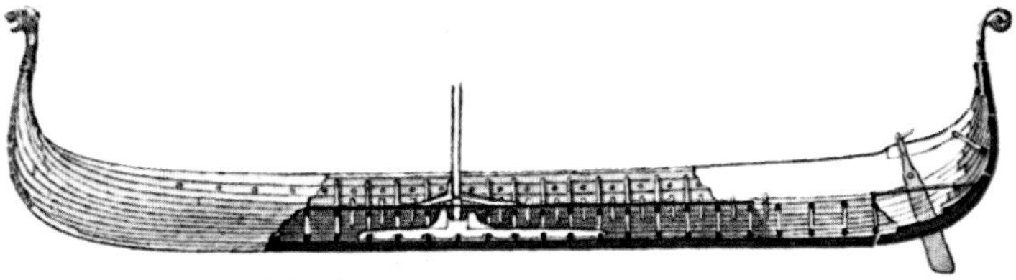

▼ *Clinker-built ships have overlapping planks. The joints were stuffed with rope to make them watertight.*

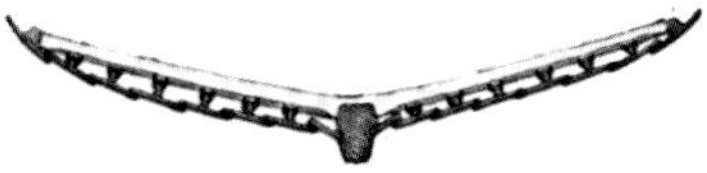

▼ *The planks were firmly fixed to a framework of ribs and crossbeams.*

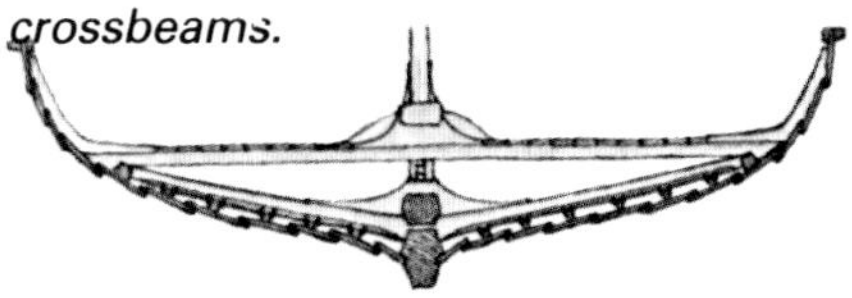

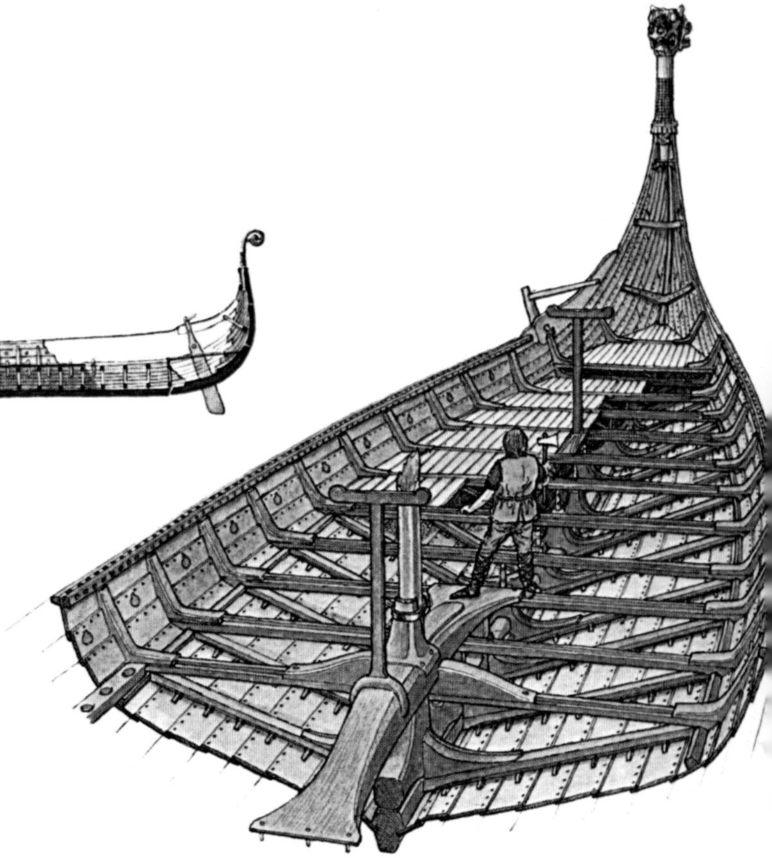

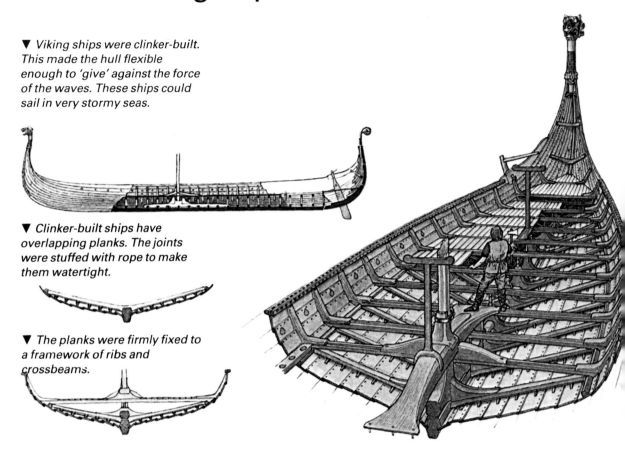

The merchant ship

◀ *A merchant ship like this was found in Roskilde Fiord in Denmark. It was broader than a warship and its planks were nailed, not lashed, to the frames. It was a sailing ship which could also be rowed.*

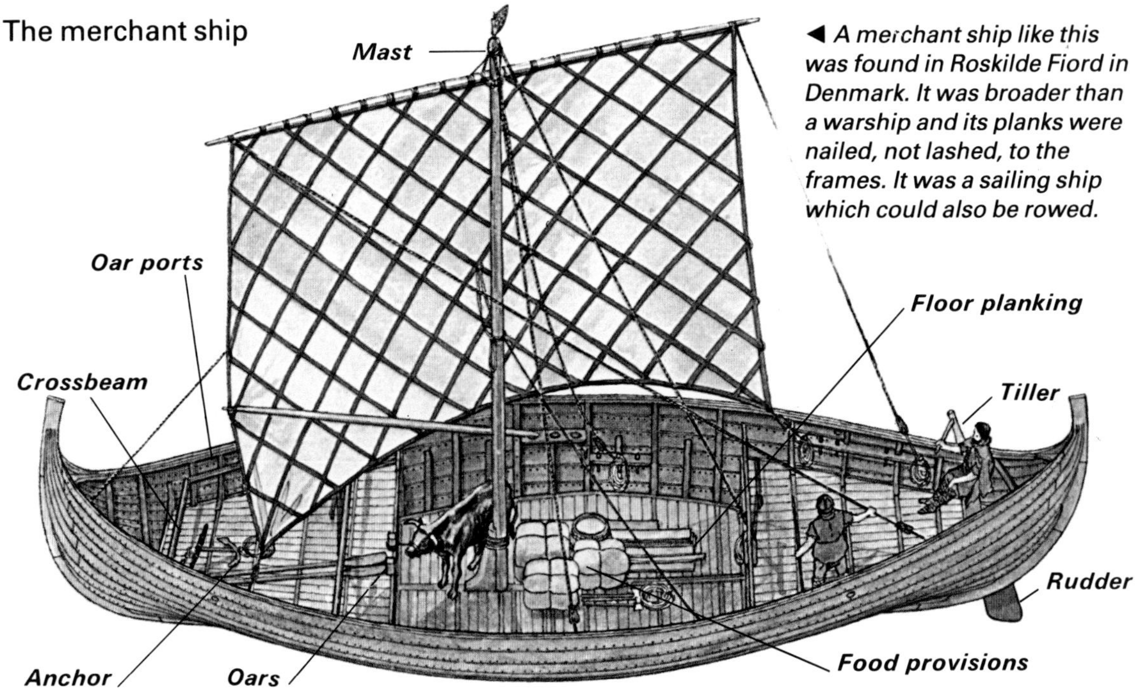

Mast
Oar ports
Floor planking
Crossbeam
Tiller
Rudder
Food provisions
Anchor
Oars

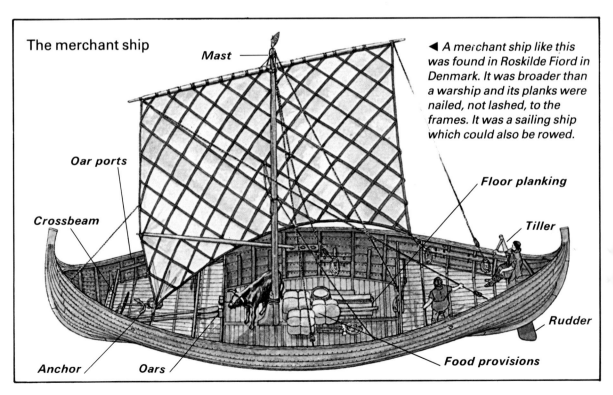

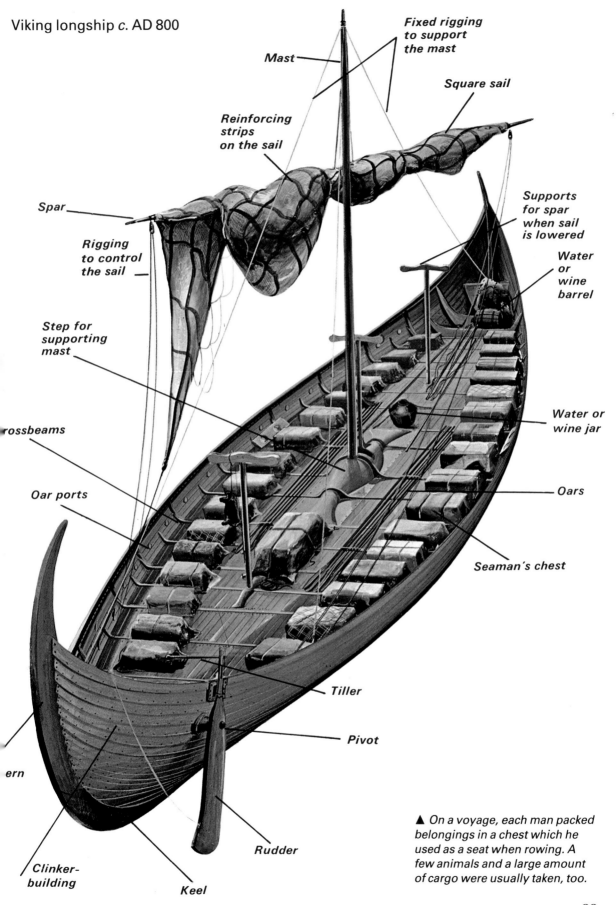

Viking longship *c*. AD 800

Mast

Fixed rigging to support the mast

Square sail

Reinforcing strips on the sail

Spar

Supports for spar when sail is lowered

Water or wine barrel

Rigging to control the sail

Step for supporting mast

Water or wine jar

rossbeams

Oar ports

Oars

Seaman's chest

Tiller

Pivot

ern

Rudder

Clinker-building

Keel

▲ *On a voyage, each man packed belongings in a chest which he used as a seat when rowing. A few animals and a large amount of cargo were usually taken, too.*

33

Hunters and fishermen

The Vikings were expert hunters and fishermen. They hunted forest animals, marsh and coastland birds and fished for river and sea fish. Sea mammals, such as seals, walruses and whales, were the biggest game. Hunting and fishing went on, wherever possible, all year round.

People living in forest areas knew the 'spoor' or footprints of the forest animals and their drinking and sleeping places. They tracked the animals down and killed them with their spears or bows and arrows. Around the marshes and coasts there were many wild ducks, geese and sea birds. These birds were probably netted and their eggs stolen from the nests.

The Vikings used baited lines, traps and nets to catch salmon and trout in streams and lakes. They speared fish in clear, shallow pools. They caught sea fish in the fiords and offshore channels along the Norwegian coast and Baltic Sea.

The Viking diet

These were some of the foods available to the Vikings. they rarely suffered from famine, but seldom had surplus food. A whale provided clothing, food, fat and oil.

Fish and shellfish

Seaweed

Meat

Mushrooms

Bread

Hare and game

Dairy produce

Onions and leeks

Nuts and berries

Poultry

Apples

Eggs

▲ *Seals and walruses could be caught in nets or speared, but whales were driven on to the shore.*

New lands in the west

While some Vikings were raiding in Europe, others were exploring westward. In about 860 Gardar Svavarson, a Swedish Viking, was blown by a storm to the coast of Iceland. Some fifteen years later the first settlers started arriving. By 930 there were about 50,000 people living in Iceland.

In 982 Erik the Red sailed westwards from Iceland and discovered a larger island. He called it Greenland to make it sound attractive to settlers. Two colonies grew up, one in the east, the other in the west. Eventually there were about 3,000 settlers in Greenland.

According to the sagas, Bjarni, an Icelander, glimpsed land to the west of Greenland. About fifteen years later Leif Erikson sailed west and discovered Helluland, Markland and Vinland. Historians think they are modern Baffin Island, Labrador and Newfoundland. For years no one knew if the sagas were based on fact. Then, in 1962, a Viking settlement dating from around AD 1000 was discovered at L'Anse-aux-Meadows in Newfoundland. This seems to prove that the Vikings reached North America.

Viking exploration westwards

Helluland

Markland

L'Anse-aux-Meadows

Vinland

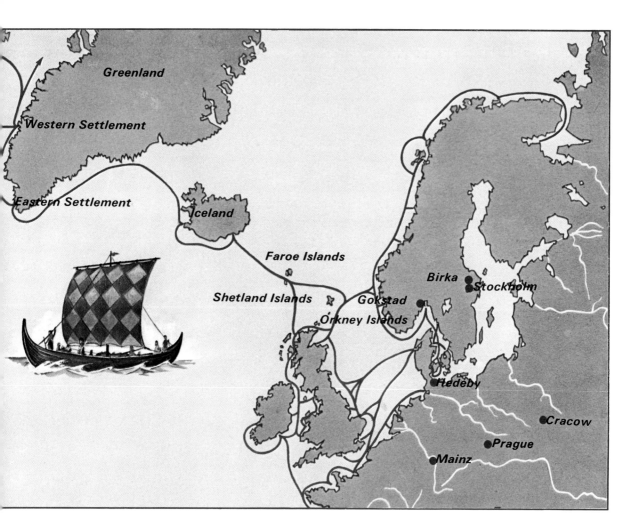

Greenland

Western Settlement

Eastern Settlement

Iceland

Faroe Islands

Shetland Islands

Gokstad

Orkney Islands

Birka

Stockholm

Hedeby

Cracow

Prague

Mainz

▲ This map shows the routes the Vikings probably took westwards across the Atlantic. We do not know the exact routes, but, because of the winds and currents, these are the most likely.

◄ The sagas tell how the Indians offered the Vikings furs and skins in exchange for red cloth and weapons. The Vikings would not sell their weapons. The Indians attacked the camp and drove the Vikings out.

► The deadly icebergs in the north Atlantic were a great danger to the Vikings' ships.

Merciless raiders

Viking raids were feared throughout Europe. The sight of a Viking ship sailing along a coast or up a river was dreaded by thousands of people. They knew that a Viking raid would leave many of them dead, their homes destroyed and their treasures stolen.

The great age of the Viking raiders lasted from 790 to 880. After that many Vikings settled in the lands they attacked. Even so, raiding continued until about 1100. By the 860s, the Vikings had permanent bases abroad, so could stay away from Scandinavia for years at a time.

The raiders were usually farmers or full-time soldiers. Generally it was the Norwegians who raided the Scottish Islands, Scotland, Ireland, north-west England and the Mediterranean. The Danes attacked eastern England, Germany, the Netherlands and France, and the Swedes raided Russia and lands to the south.

1 *Hastein led a famous raid between 859 and 862. He left France with 62 ships.*

4 *After a successful raid in France, they sailed for Italy. When they saw the magnificent city of Luna, they thought it was Rome. They attacked the city but were beaten back.*

5 *Then Hastein pretended to be dying. He was baptized by one of the priests of Luna.*

2 *He sailed south to Spain where he was defeated by the Arabs. He managed to enter the*

Mediterranean and plundered the coast of north Africa and Spain.

3 *The Vikings spent the winter on an island at the mouth of the river Rhone.*

6 *Hastein's coffin was carried by Vikings into the town cemetery.*

7 *Once in the town, Hastein leapt out of his coffin and his men drew their weapons. They looted*

the place and Hastein and his Vikings returned to France laden with treasure.

The warrior and his weapons

The Vikings were fierce warriors and had some of the best armour and weapons in Europe. They wore tough leather tunics, occasionally with chain-mail shirts over them. They wore simple conical helmets, not the winged helmets so often drawn by artists. They carried large round wooden shields which were painted and sometimes covered with leather.

The Vikings' usual weapons were swords, spears and axes. Their long swords were sharpened along both edges. They used two types of spear: light throwing ones and heavy thrusting ones. The axes were powerful weapons and could cut off an enemy's hands, feet or head. Bows and arrows were sometimes used to shoot enemies at long range.

The Vikings were extremely successful warriors, although they were defeated by the Arabs, Anglo-Saxons and Irish at various times.

▼ *The Vikings built fine defensive fortifications. Four have been excavated in Denmark. They all date from the late tenth or early eleventh centuries. They may have been used either as training bases or as places of refuge for soldiers.*

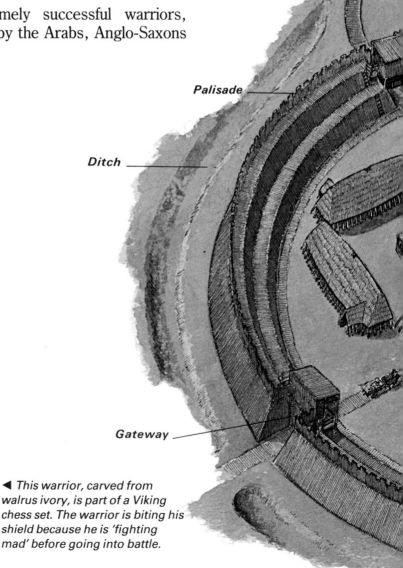

Palisade

Ditch

Gateway

◄ *This warrior, carved from walrus ivory, is part of a Viking chess set. The warrior is biting his shield because he is 'fighting mad' before going into battle.*

▲ This shield was made of wooden boards. Shields were sometimes painted or covered with leather. The round metal casing, or boss, in the middle protected the fingers.

▲ Soldiers wore simple conical helmets like this one, shown on a carving from Sigtuna in Sweden.

▲ Only the wealthier soldiers could afford a mail shirt like this. They were passed on from father to son.

Living quarters

Earth rampart 17 metres thick, 7 metres high

The role of women

Viking women were responsible for all the household duties: cooking, cleaning, washing and looking after the children. They also made the family's clothes from the wool they had earlier spun into thread and woven into cloth.

Viking women could be very independent, especially if they came from a wealthy family. They could own land and other valuables and act as farmers and traders in their own right. In many countries at this time women were not allowed to do these things.

It was usually the women who taught their children stories, poetry and riddles. In this way they made sure that traditions were passed on. Few people could read or write, so this was the only way the Vikings had of passing on knowledge.

▶ Sometimes the Vikings carved scenes from important people's lives on large stones. This imaginary picture stone tells the story of the life of Aud the Deep Minded, widow of King Olaf the White of Dublin. At the bottom, Aud is shown at the wedding of her grand-daughter, where there is feasting and rejoicing. Aud then sets sail for Iceland in her merchant ship. She buys land, and is shown in the top picture directing the ploughing and cultivation of her farmstead. When she dies, she is placed in a burial ship and covered with a huge mound of earth.

▲ When two people married, the man had to pay the bride's father a 'brideprice'. This was a gift of cattle or gold.

▲ If a couple wanted to divorce they only had to tell some witnesses that they wished to separate.

▲ The woman looked after the farmstead if her husband was away. She would defend their home against attack.

▲ Women traded with visiting merchants when their husbands were away on a raid or if they were widows.

43

Death of a hero

When a Viking warrior died, he was buried with great splendour. His body was dressed in his best clothes and jewellery and laid in the grave. His weapons, tools and most precious possessions were placed beside him. The richer the Viking, the more magnificent his grave. Wealthy people were buried in great wooden chambers with their favourite horse and dog and large quantities of food and drink. Scholars think these possessions were to help the man on his journey after death. Some Viking chieftains were buried in their ships.

▼ *The Vikings believed that as soon as the body was burnt the spirit went to Valhalla. This was a heaven where warriors spent their time fighting and feastig. Warriors hoped to reach Valhalla by dying with a sword in their hand.*

An Arab called Ibn Fadlan who watched a ship burial in Russia described what he saw. At the king's burial place he saw a fine ship drawn up on dry land and surrounded with firewood. The ship was full of beautiful armour, weapons, carved chairs and beds. The body of the king was carried to the ship and laid on a couch. Then some horses, cows and dogs were sacrificed and their bodies thrown on to the ship. Lastly, a relative of the dead man stepped forward from the silent crowd and set light to the wood with a blazing torch. In a moment everything was ablaze. The ashes left by the fire were covered with a mound of earth. Sometimes these burial ships were buried and not burnt. Many have been discovered by archaeologists, and have provided a great deal of information about the Vikings.

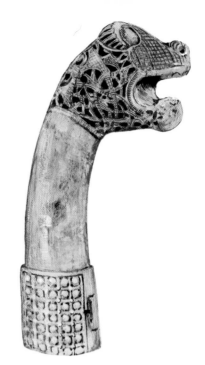

▲ This lion-headed post was one of four found on the Oseberg ship. It was probably to frighten off evil spirits.

◄ The Norwegian Oseberg ship was excavated in 1904. It was covered with a mound of peat, which had preserved it.

► The waggon from the Oseberg ship is the only one found. Its sides are carved with scenes from Norse myths.

45

Norse gods and legends

The Vikings believed that the world was ruled by gods who lived in a heavenly place called Asgard. The greatest of their gods was Odin. He was wise, cunning and dangerous and filled everyone with fear. He was only seen in battles or at other times of great danger. Only those who believed they had supernatural power dared worship him.

Thor was a very different god. He carried a huge stone hammer called Mjollnir. Thor was the god of wind, rain and farming. When he drove across the sky in his enormous chariot drawn by goats, there was thunder and lightning. In spite of his tremendous strength and quick temper, Thor was a happy, rather stupid, god. Thor's day (Thursday) was the usual time for meetings and feasts.

Frey was the god of marriage and growing things. When the Vikings sowed their crops they scattered bread and poured wine or beer on to the ground. They hoped to please Frey so he would make the crops grow well.

The Vikings had no churches or temples. They usually worshipped their gods outdoors where they believed there was no danger from evil spirits.

▲ This picture stone shows Odin racing across the sky on his eight-legged horse. Sleipnir. His wolves, Geri and Freki, went with him.

▶ There are many waterfalls in Scandinavia like Latefoss in Norway. The Vikings may have worshipped their gods beside waterfalls.

▲ The Valkyries were women sent by Odin to lead dead warriors to Valhalla, the Viking heaven.

▲ This bronze image of Frey, the god of fertility, was found in Sweden.

▲ This model of Thor's hammer would have been worn by a Viking as protection against evil spirits.

The final battle

The Vikings told the stories of their heroes in sagas. These sagas were passed down from one generation to the next by word of mouth. They were not written down until the thirteenth century, long after the events they described. One of the greatest saga writers was Snorri Sturluson, who lived in Iceland. He wrote a series of stories called *Heimskringla*, which means *The Wreath of the World*. One of the heroes of these stories were King Harald Hardrada of Norway.

Harald left Norway after his half-brother, King Olaf, was killed. He went to the Mediterranean and after much raiding and looting, joined the Viking guard of the emperor in Constantinople.

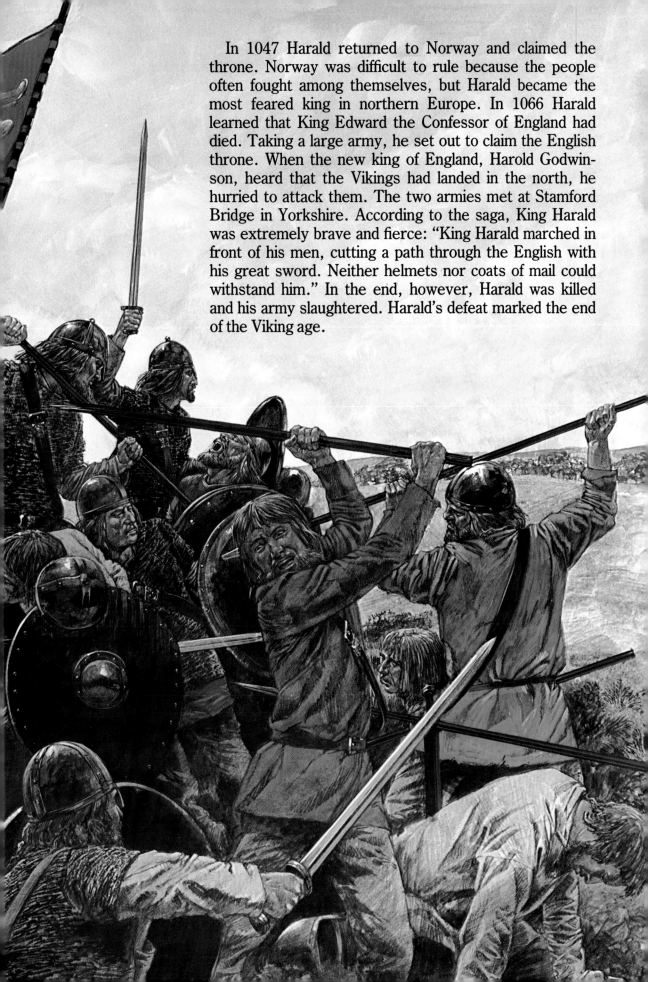

In 1047 Harald returned to Norway and claimed the throne. Norway was difficult to rule because the people often fought among themselves, but Harald became the most feared king in northern Europe. In 1066 Harald learned that King Edward the Confessor of England had died. Taking a large army, he set out to claim the English throne. When the new king of England, Harold Godwinson, heard that the Vikings had landed in the north, he hurried to attack them. The two armies met at Stamford Bridge in Yorkshire. According to the saga, King Harald was extremely brave and fierce: "King Harald marched in front of his men, cutting a path through the English with his great sword. Neither helmets nor coats of mail could withstand him." In the end, however, Harald was killed and his army slaughtered. Harald's defeat marked the end of the Viking age.

The Viking sunset

The Viking raids came to an end around 1100. However, Scandinavians continued to trade in Europe and to sail to North America to cut timber. At home, the Vikings tended to lead a more settled life, fighting far less.

Slowly, the kings of Norway, Sweden and Denmark were each uniting their country. As a result people fought each other less and devoted more time to agriculture and other crafts and skills. This made the countries more prosperous and people were not so keen to leave their homes to fight. They were happy to be farmers and craftsmen.

By the beginning of the eleventh century, the Vikings found it harder to attack Germany, Holland, France and England. Strong armies and fleets were waiting for them, and some countries even used Vikings to defend them. Rollo and his men, for example, guarded the northern shores of France.

During the tenth and eleventh centuries, many Vikings were converted to Christianity. They had to abandon their own gods, which they had worshipped for hundreds of years, in favour of Christian beliefs. These changed the Vikings' way of life and lessened their power.

▲ *This is one of the oldest crucifixes yet found in Scandinavia. Dating from the tenth century, it was discovered at Birka in Sweden.*

▶ *King Harald Bluetooth of Denmark was baptized in 960. He became a Christian after seeing a missionary pick up a red-hot iron bar without burning himself.*

Legacy of the Vikings

For many years people regarded the Vikings as brutal barbarians who did nothing but loot and kill. This was not so.

The Vikings were great traders. Wherever they went they built new towns or enlarged old ones, like Kiev in Russia and Dublin in Ireland. They took furs and slaves to Constantinople and Baghdad and returned with silks, spices, precious metals and wines. They were also great explorers, and travelled as far as the Scottish Islands, Iceland, Greenland and North America. In many of these places, such as Iceland and Greenland, they founded permanent settlements.

Although the Vikings were fierce and quarrelsome, they believed in law and order. The *Althing*, an assembly which was partly a parliament and partly a law court, was the first such institution in Europe. The Viking warriors also valued their freedom. When a messenger asked to be taken to the leader of Rollo's army he was told that there was no leader, everyone was equal.

The Vikings were great artists. They decorated their weapons, furniture and houses with beautiful designs and pictures. They worked equally well in wood, iron, horn and ivory. Their boat-building skills enabled them to sail the Atlantic quite safely.

Sagas were stories passed down by word of mouth until they were finally written down by scholars in the thirteenth century. This extract describes the Battle of Svolder in 1000, in which the brave King Olaf of Norway was defeated by King Swein of Denmark and King Olov of Sweden.

"*The battle was fierce and bitter. Olaf's men threw grappling irons on to Swein's ships, but King Swein and his men escaped on to their other ships and retreated. Then King Olov came alongside and attacked, but he suffered the same fate as the others, losing many men and several ships.*

But at last, all King Olaf's ships were captured except the Long Serpent. *There was such a hail of arrows and spears that Olaf's men were unable to protect themselves. King Olaf now had so few men that the enemy were able to board his ship. His crew were forced to jump overboard, where they were killed by the enemy.*

Then, King Olaf himself leapt into the water. They tried to seize him, but the king raised his shield above his head and sank forever beneath the waves."

The story of the Vikings

793

This is the accepted date of the first Viking attack on western Europe. A band of Vikings attacked and destroyed the famous monastery of Lindisfarne off the north-east coast of England. For a time the Vikings on the Continent were held in check by the great emperor Charlemagne (742–814). When he died, his empire broke up and Viking attacks began.

830

Viking fleets sailed up the rivers and over the seas into Holland, France, England and Ireland. Later they attacked Spain, but found the Moslem Moors fiercer than themselves. This did not stop them entering the Mediterranean. They even sailed to the eastern Mediterranean and looted coastal towns there.

While the Norwegians and Danes were attacking western Europe and the Mediterranean, the Swedes moved into Russia. They founded and settled in towns close to the great Russian rivers and built up a rich trade with Constantinople. Some of them crossed Russia

▲ The Vikings attacking the Byzantines at Constantinople.

and sailed down the River Volga to the Caspian Sea. Here, they traded with Arab merchants from Baghdad. For some time the Varangian Vikings, as they were called, repeatedly raided these cities. However, the Byzantines and the Arabs were too powerful for them.

▲ King Alfred flees in the face of Viking attack.

851

The Danes set up a base on the Isle of Sheppey in the Thames and wintered in England. They were no longer content to make lightning raids on Europe. They were now determined to carry out concentrated attacks and set up similar bases on islands in French and German rivers.

878

In England, Wessex was one of the last Anglo-Saxon states free from Viking rule. The Danes, led by Guthrum, invaded Wessex and seized control. King Alfred was forced to flee to the Isle of Athelney in Somerset until he could collect his army together. Then he defeated the Danes at the Battle of Edington. He made peace and allowed the Danes to continue living in eastern England. This area was called the Danelaw.

892

The 'Great Army' crossed the Channel to England. For four years the Vikings tried to overcome King Alfred's resistance. Finally the king triumphed, and the army left the country in 896.

King Charles the Fat invited Rollo and his men to settle in Normandy to defend its shores against other Scandinavians. Rollo agreed and was loyal and successful.

▲ *King Charles the Fat invites Rollo to settle in Normandy.*

982

In 982, Erik the Red set sail from Iceland and sighted a rocky and unpromising land. He called this country 'Greenland' to attract settlers. In 986, a sailor called Bjarni was blown off course and sighted a land to the west of Greenland. No one tried to explore this new land until Leif Erikson set out. He reached Helluland (Baffin Island), Markland (Labrador) and Vinland (Newfoundland).

According to the saga writers, there were several other voyages to Vinland. However, Indian attacks prevented the Vikings from founding a permanent colony in North America. Expeditions continued to go to Markland for timber until 1347.

▲ *The Indians force the Vikings to leave North America.*

1002

Another great wave of Viking attacks took place. In England, King Ethelred the Unready (or the 'ill-advised') could not decide how to deal with the Viking invaders.

Later, the king ordered his followers to murder all the Vikings they could find. It is said that Gunhild, King Swein Forkbeard's sister, was killed in this massacre. Certainly, Swein raided England even more often and finally conquered it. His son Knut, or Canute, ruled the country between 1017 and 1035. Knut forced the Vikings and English to live peacefully together. In 1030, Knut defeated and killed King Olaf of Norway at the Battle of Stiklestad and became the master of a huge Scandinavian empire. Unfortunately, his sons were not strong enough to rule it after his death and the empire collapsed.

1066

By this time the Scandinavian world was relatively quiet and peaceful. King Harald Hardrada attacked England but was killed at the Battle of Stamford Bridge. The Viking age was over.

Famous Vikings

Rollo (860–931) became the first Viking Duke of Normandy. He was originally called Rolf the Ganger or Walker. This was because his legs were so long that he could not find a horse big enough to carry him. He spent ten years attacking France before King Charles the Fat offered him land to settle on in France. In return, he defended France against all other Scandinavians. In 912, he became a Christian. William the Conqueror was one of his descendants.

Hakon I (915–960) was the first Christian king of Norway. He was educated at the court of King Athelstan of England. He returned to Norway in 935 and claimed the throne. He introduced Christianity and tried to establish law and order by setting up *things* all over Norway. He was killed in battle in 960.

Harald Bluetooth (?–986) was a king of Denmark. In the late 950s he attacked Norway. At first, King Hakon defeated him but in 960 Harald killed his rival and became king of both Denmark and Norway. Worse still, in 974, he was attacked by the armies of the German emperor, Otto II. Soon afterwards, Harald was overthrown by his ambitious son, Swein Forkbeard, and died in exile in 986.

Swein Forkbeard (960–1014) was one of the most successful kings of Denmark. He cleared the Germans out of Jutland and set about raiding his neighbours. In 994, he took part in a great attack on England. At the Battle of Svolder in 1000, he defeated and killed Olaf Tryggvason, the king of Norway. After the Massacre of St Brice's Day in 1002, Swein spent much of his time in England. He died at Gainsborough in Lincolnshire in 1014.

▲ *A statue of Rollo, later Duke of Normandy.*

Olaf Tryggvason (968–1000) was a famous king of Norway who made his name by attacking England. In 994 he attacked London with Swein Forkbeard, but without success. He became a Christian and was made King of Norway on his return. He tried hard to convert his people to Christianity, but was unsuccessful. Unfortunately, he quarrelled with Swein Forkbeard and was killed at the Battle of Svolder in 1000.

St Olaf (?–1030) seized control of Norway on the death of Swein Forkbeard in 1014. In 1016 he was accepted as king and devoted himself to the task of converting his people to Christianity. He was defeated in 1026 at the Battle of the River Helge. In 1028 Knut invaded Norway and Olaf fled to Russia. He was killed fighting bravely at the Battle of Stiklestad.

Knut the Great or Canute (?995–1035) was probably the greatest of the Viking kings. He continued the work of Swein Forkbeard, his father, in England and was recognized as king in 1017. For the rest of his life he managed to persuade the Saxons and Vikings in England to live in peace. He made many wise laws. He defeated Olaf of Norway at the Battle of Stiklestad in 1030 and became King of Norway. When he died, his empire collapsed because of the weakness of his sons.

▲ Leif Erikson, discoverer of America.

Harald Hardrada (1015–1066) was present at the Battle of Stiklestad and saw the king, his half-brother, die. He fled to Russia and made his way to the Mediterranean world. There he lived first as a pirate and then as a member of the Byzantine emperor's guard. In 1047 he returned to Norway and claimed the throne. However, it was many years before all the Norwegians accepted him. He led an expedition to England in 1066 and was killed at the Battle of Stamford Bridge by Harold Godwinson, King of England.

Erik the Red (?–1000) was brought up in south-west Norway but was outlawed for killing a man. He sailed to Iceland and made his home there. But, once again, he was banished for murder. As both Iceland and Norway were closed to him, he sailed westwards in search of a land first sighted fifty years earlier by a sailor called Gunnbjorn. In 982, Erik came across a huge, rocky land. For the next three years he explored its coasts. Then he returned to Iceland and collected together a large group of settlers. In 986 he led a fleet of 25 ships to what he called 'Greenland'. This was the start of a flourishing colony. Erik ran a successful farm at Brattahlid in south-western Greenland until his death.

Leif Erikson (?–?) was the eldest son of Erik the Red. In about 1000, he decided to go in search of a mysterious land sighted by an Icelander called Bjarni in 986. As a result, he discovered Helluland (modern Baffin Island), Markland (Labrador) and Vinland (Newfoundland). On his return to Greenland he learned that his father had died. He gave up exploring and took over the running of the family farm at Brattahlid.

The world the Vikings knew

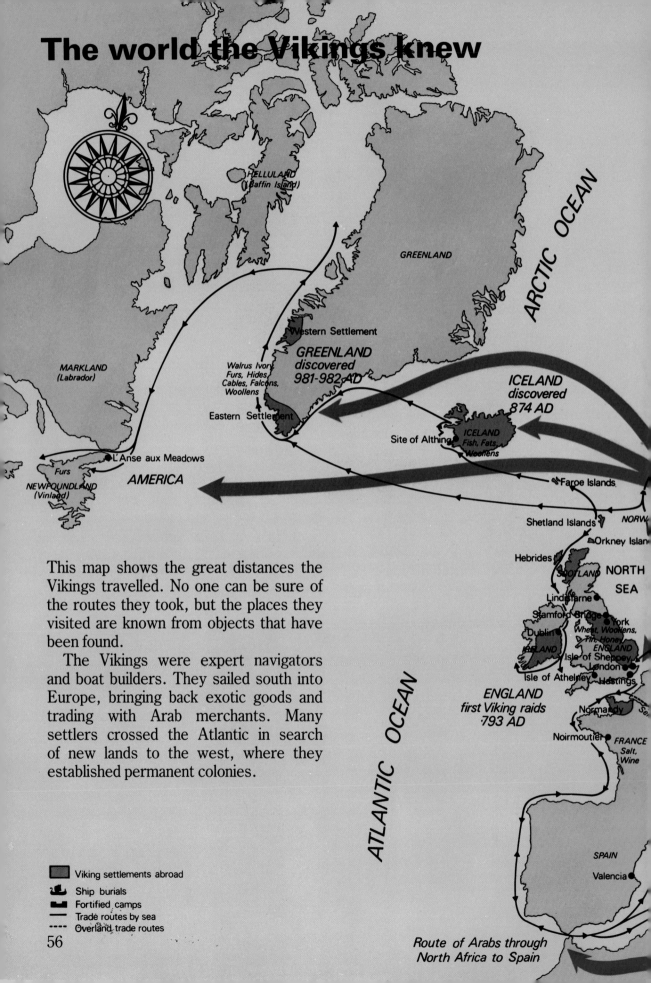

HELLULAND
(Baffin Island)

ARCTIC OCEAN

GREENLAND

Western Settlement

GREENLAND
discovered
981-982 AD

MARKLAND
(Labrador)

Walrus Ivory,
Furs, Hides,
Cables, Falcons,
Woollens

ICELAND
discovered
874 AD

Eastern Settlement

Site of Althing

ICELAND
Fish, Fats,
Woollens

L'Anse aux Meadows

Furs

AMERICA

Faroe Islands

NEWFOUNDLAND
(Vinland)

Shetland Islands

NORW

Orkney Islan

Hebrides

NORTH
SEA

SCOTLAND

This map shows the great distances the
Vikings travelled. No one can be sure of
the routes they took, but the places they
visited are known from objects that have
been found.

Lindisfarne

Stamford Bridge

York

Dublin

Wheat, Woollens,
Tin, Honey

The Vikings were expert navigators
and boat builders. They sailed south into
Europe, bringing back exotic goods and
trading with Arab merchants. Many
settlers crossed the Atlantic in search
of new lands to the west, where they
established permanent colonies.

IRELAND

ENGLAND

Isle of Sheppey

London

Isle of Athelney

Hastings

ENGLAND
first Viking raids
793 AD

Normandy

Se

Noirmoutier

FRANCE
Salt,
Wine

ATLANTIC OCEAN

SPAIN

Valencia

Viking settlements abroad

Ship burials

Fortified camps

Trade routes by sea

Overland trade routes

56

*Route of Arabs through
North Africa to Spain*

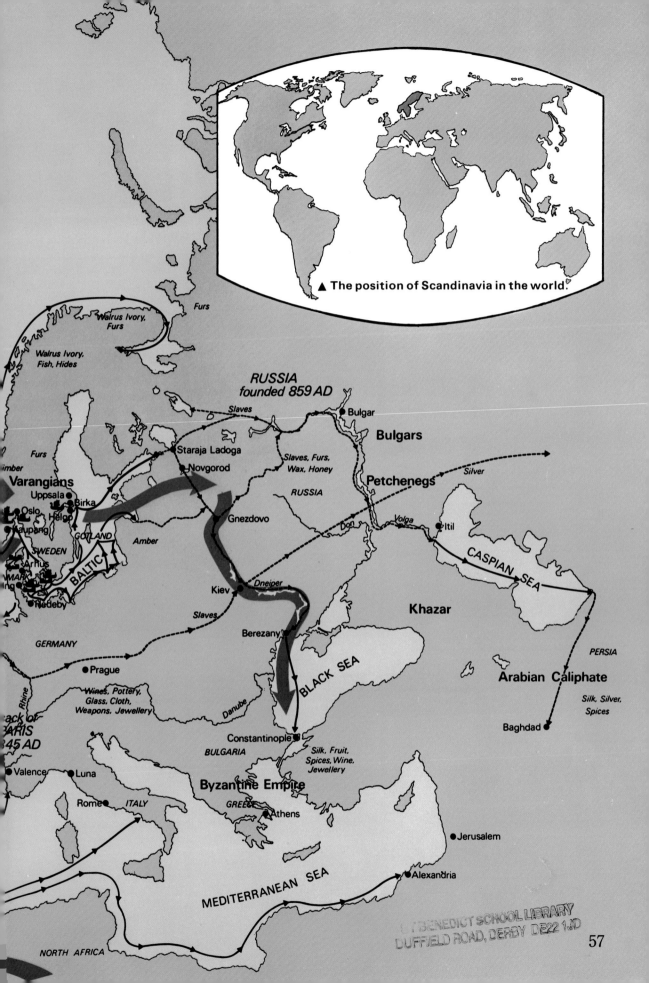

▲ The position of Scandinavia in the world.

Furs

Walrus Ivory, Furs

Walrus Ivory, Fish, Hides

Furs

RUSSIA
founded 859 AD

Slaves

● Bulgar

Bulgars

Staraja Ladoga ●
● Novgorod

Slaves, Furs, Wax, Honey

Petchenegs

Silver

Varangians

Uppsala ●
● Birka

RUSSIA

Gnezdovo ●

Don

Volga

● Iltil

Oslo ● ● Helgo
● Kaupang

GOTLAND

Amber

SWEDEN

CASPIAN SEA

Århus

MARK
● Hedeby

BALTIC

Kiev ●

Dneiper

Khazar

Slaves

Berezany ●

GERMANY

● Prague

PERSIA

Rhine

Wines, Pottery, Glass, Cloth, Weapons, Jewellery

Danube

BLACK SEA

Arabian Caliphate

ack of
ARIS
45 AD

Silk, Silver, Spices

Baghdad ●

● Valence
● Luna

Constantinople ●

BULGARIA

Silk, Fruit, Spices, Wine, Jewellery

Rome ●
ITALY

Byzantine Empire

GREECE
● Athens

● Jerusalem

MEDITERRANEAN SEA

● Alexandria

NORTH AFRICA

57

World history AD 800 to 1100

	Vikings	Europe	Asia

AD	Vikings	Europe	Asia
800	Traditionally, Lindisfarne was the first place in Europe to be attacked by the Vikings (793). After that, Germany, the Netherlands, France and the British Isles suffered almost continuous attack.	Charlemagne, king of the Franks, was crowned Holy Roman Emperor by the Pope (800). He created a large empire, including France, Germany and northern Italy. His sons quarrelled and divided the empire in 847. Their wars gave the Vikings the chance to attack Europe.	The Tang dynasty ruled China from 611 to 907. During that time China enjoyed a 'Golden Age' in art. Poetry, painting and porcelain reached particularly high standards in Japan, the Fujiwara family controlled the emperor between the mid-ninth and the twelfth centuries.
860	National monarchies appeared in Norway, Denmark and Sweden, Halvdan united Norway (850) and Gorm united Denmark (860). The Swedish Vikings invaded Russia and took over the Slav cities of Novgorod and Kiev (862).	The Bulgars in eastern Europe were converted to Christianity (861). The Macedonian emperors ruled the Byzantine empire from 867 to 1056. Siegfried, king of the Danes, besieged Paris (885–886). Rollo became Duke of Normandy.	A great empire grew up in the Mekong Valley in south-east Asia. It was ruled by the Hindu Khmers. Angkor was the capital of this empire. It was full of fine temples decorated with splendid carvings.
920	Harald Bluetooth of Denmark became a Christian, as did Hakon the Good of Norway. Harald invaded Norway and killed Hakon in 960.	Otto I united Germany and northern Italy. He was crowned emperor in 962. He also managed to defeat the Magyars, the wild horsemen from the steppes, who eventually settled in Hungary.	India was divided up into a number of states. Perhaps the most important people were the Rajputs who spread widely over central and northern India. Buddhism spread rapidly from India to China and Japan
980	Swein Forkbeard of Denmark defeated and killed Olaf Tryggvason of Norway at the Battle of Svolder (1000). The Massacre of St Brice's Day (1002) led to the conquest of England by Swein and Knut of Denmark. In 1028, Knut killed King Olaf and added Norway to his empire.	Basil II, the Byzantine emperor, defeated the Bulgars and destroyed their power (1014). Normans arrived in southern Italy and fought the Byzantines. Robert Guiscard was one of their greatest leaders. They made themselves masters of southern Italy and Sicily.	The Sung dynasty (960–1279) came to power in China. The Sung were also famous for their art and inventions. They invented the abacus, printing blocks, and movable type. They produced a fine encyclopedia and made hand-grenades out of gunpowder.
1040	The Swedes were converted to Christianity and King Harald Hardrada of Norway made the last great Viking raid. He attacked England in 1066 and was defeated and killed at the Battle of Stamford Bridge.	El Cid, Spain's national hero, steadily pushed back the Moslem Moors (1040–1099). Pope Gregory VII and the emperor Henry IV quarrelled over the appointment of bishops (1076). Pope Urban II preached the first crusade at Clermont (1095).	The Sung administration was particularly efficient. Anyone wanting to be a civil servant had to pass three sets of exams. Even then only the very best graduates were chosen. Later, Europeans called these civil servants *mandarins*.

Africa	Near East	America	
			AD
The central Sudan was dominated by the great empire of Kanem which lasted from 800 to 1400. It was a highly centralized empire with powerful armies.	A new dynasty of caliphs called the Abbasids took over the Arab empire in 750. They made Baghdad their capital. It became a great centre of trade. Spices and minerals came from India, jewels and fabrics from central Asia, ivory and gold from Africa and silks and porcelain from China.	The Mayas, who lived in Guatemala, Yucatan and south-east Mexico, came to the end of their classical period. They built magnificent stone cities but probably did not live in them. They were only used for religious purposes.	800
			AD
During the ninth century an unknown people built the city of Zimbabwe in Rhodesia. The ruins consist of walled huts and enclosures with conical towers and gigantic walls.	The Arabs made great discoveries in the world of medicine. For example, Al Razi (860-935) discovered many ways of treating measles and smallpox. He wrote 200 text books before he died. In mathematics, the Arabs brought the numerals 1-9 from India and introduced 0.	The Mayan civilization suffered widespread decline, coming to an end in parts of Mexico and Guatemala. However, they continued to flourish in Yucatan. The Toltecs conquered the Valley of Mexico and made Tula their capital.	860
			AD
The empire of Ghana was set up in west Africa. It was famous for gold and slaves and sold both to the people living in north Africa. The Ghanaians were Moslems and their cities contained beautiful mosques.	The Abbasid empire broke up into a number of smaller empires. For example, the Fatimids seized control of north Africa.	The Toltecs invaded the Maya empire. Although they absorbed many Mayan ideas, they were basically a race of warriors. As a result, there was a period of almost continuous war. In South America, Peru was dominated first by Tiahuanaco and then by the Chimu in the north.	920
			AD
North Africa was dominated by the Fatimids from 908 onwards. They gradually made their way east and conquered Egypt in 969. Later, they took over Palestine, Syria and Arabia. In the eleventh century the Almoravids took their place in north Africa.	The Seljuk Turks forced their way into much of what we now call the Middle East from the Russian steppes. In 1038 they invaded Persia and seized Baghdad (1058). The Seljuks swept all before them and decided to attack the Byzantine empire.	The warlike Toltecs conquered many smaller, independent states, and became rulers of most of west Mexico. Chichen Itza became a Toltec city.	980
			AD
The Almoravids conquered west Africa and converted many of the people to the Moslem religion. Towards 1100 the Yoruba empire was created near the mouth of the river Niger. The people reached a high level of civilization and made exquisite bronzes.	In 1071, the Seljuks defeated the Byzantines and the emperor was forced to ask the Pope and the rulers of western Europe for help. The crusaders conquered the Holy Land but refused to hand it over to the Byzantines. Instead, they set up states of their own.	The Miztec tribe expanded under the leadership of their chief, Eight-Deer Ocelot Claw. In Peru, the Chimu people created a coastal empire, six hundred miles long. The city of Tula was destroyed by invading northern tribes.	1040 AD 1100

Glossary　　Index